The Jane Poems

Also by Ronald Moran

Poetry (Books and Chapbooks)

Waiting
The Blurring of Time
Diagramming the Clear Sky
Saying These Things
Greatest Hits, 1965-2000
Fish Out of Water
Getting the Body to Dance Again
Sudden Fictions
Life on the Rim
So Simply Means the Rain

Criticism

Four Poets and the Emotive Imagination (with co-author)
Louis Simpson

The Jane Poems

Ronald Moran

Copyright 2011 by Ronald Moran
ISBN 978-0-9842598-5-4

Published by Clemson University Press in Clemson, South Carolina

Editorial Assistant: Emily Kudeviz

Front cover photograph of Jane (taken at "The Little Church Around the Corner," New York City, on January 31, 1959) and photographs on p. 40 are courtesy of the poet.

Cover designer: Christine Cook

To order copies, please visit the Clemson University Press website: www.clemson.edu/press

Contents

Acknowledgments vii
Dedication viii

ॐ

Part One
At the Lincoln Diner 2
The Courtship 3
A Poem for Jane 4
Interloper 5
Double Passage in Mid-Life 6
A Night on the Road 7
Through an Upstairs Window 8
Weddings 9
Room by Room 10
Sound Waves 11
Dress Codes 12

Part Two
Flight Patterns 14
The Prize 15
Mirrors 16
At the Kitchen Table 17
Tic Tacs 18
Sounds of a Late Afternoon 19
Saying These Things 20
Jane 21
Foreplay 22
What I Can Do from Here 23
Surgical Waiting Room 24
The Breakdown 25
Golden Anniversary 27
A Clearing Over Caesars Head 28
The Frame 29

The Hand 30
South on the Interstate 31
A Blessing 32
Allergic Reaction 33
Waking up Tired 34
Night Calls 35
Dark House 36
Pain 37
Fear and Love 38
Roots 39

Part Three
Lines of Demarcation 42
In Place of a Prayer 43
The Reprimand 44
Mother and Daughter 45
Killing Time 46
The Wait 47
Living Space 48
Letters to Jane 49
Trying to Stay Alive 52
On Going to See a Bereavement Counselor for the First Time
on an Afternoon in Mid-July 53
The Language of Holding Up 54
Trying to Make Peace 55
Pillows 56
November 23, 2009 57
Learning How 58

A Note on the Author 60

Acknowledgments

The poems identified below appeared in earlier collections of my poetry, and I thank the publishers for their cooperation in permitting the poems to be reprinted here: "A Poem for Jane," "A Walk on A Summer Day," and "Interloper" from *So Simply Means the Rain*, Claitor's Book Store, 1965; "Life on the Rim "and "Double Passage in Mid-Life" from *Life on the Rim*, Juniper Press, 1988; "Dress Codes" and "Fish Out of Water" from *Fish Out of Water*, Juniper Press, 2000; "A Night on the Road," "Foreplay," "Jane," "Room by Room," "Saying These Things," "Surgical Waiting Room," "Through an Upstairs Window," "Weddings," and "What I Can Do from Here" from *Saying These Things*, Clemson University Digital Press, 2003; "Allergic Reaction," "At the Kitchen Table," "Flight Patterns," "Sounds of a Late Afternoon," "The Courtship," "The Prize," and "Tic Tacs" from *The Blurring of Time*, Clemson University Digital Press, 2007; "A Blessing," "A Clearing Over Caesars Head," "At the Lincoln Diner," "Night Calls," "South on the Interstate," and "Waking Up Tired" from *Waiting*, Clemson University Digital Press, 2009.

Of the new poems for which this represents the first book publication, the following poems appeared first in the following publications: "Killing Time," *Abbey*; "The Language of Holding Up," *Emrys Journal*; "The Wait," *Evening Street Review* ; "In Place of a Prayer," "Lines of Demarcation," and "On Going to See a Bereavement Counselor for the First Time in Mid-July, 2009," *The South Carolina Review*; and "Mother and Daughter," *Stickman Review*.

Many of the poems in this book were dedicated to Jane, the dedication appearing between the title and first line. I have deleted these dedications, for the most part, given the special nature of this book. In addition, some of the poems have been very slightly altered since their original publication in journals or in earlier book form.

Dedication

This book is dedicated to the memory of Jane Moran, my wife for 50 years. Jane was born in Hartford, Connecticut, on June 13, 1938, and died in Simpsonville, South Carolina, on February 23, 2009. In addition to saving my life by marrying me, she was the love of my life, the best reader of my poetry, my best friend, and the most loved and loving person I have ever known.

A Walk on a Summer Day

This nervous boy beside me is my son.
Three years and not a yardstick high,
he quarrels with weeds, questions trucks;
anything that moves he riddles thoroughly.

Behind us, trailing back with every block,
my calm paced wife accepts the time,
the place, the storm sounds clapping in.
My son's twin sister holds her hand.

Father and son, we hunt tornadoes.
Behind us, our women walk easily.

Part One

At the Lincoln Diner

Once I was sitting in the Lincoln Diner on West Main
        with Dick Hetzler,
eating French fries doused in salt and thick ketchup,
        while across from us,

on a stool, a large-boned woman, but not plump,
        seemed happy
until we came in, or, rather, until Dick came in,
        who, after downing

his fries and shake, looked at me, then at her,
        and said loud enough,
She's not that fat, Ronnie! which spun her around
        to give me

that special look reserved for barnyard clods,
        her jaws
working overtime, a spot of mayonnaise gracing
        her full upper lip,

as her boyfriend, a big dude, sat back, flexing
        his forearms,
as if he would have liked to loosen my face but for
        Dick's being there

to complicate his mission of defending her honor;
        and Dick was laughing
so hard his eyes were wet with pleasure at my undoing,
        so I said to him,

Why'd you go and say a stupid thing like that?
        while I am thinking,
What could I possibly do to redeem myself to her,
        without making

my good buddy the fall guy, the easy-going one who
        lived on my street
and whose sister broke my heart five years later,
        then married me.

The Courtship

In the middle of the Cold War,
I lived in a bombed-out shelter
of compliance until the all clear

sounded, like the lid of a grate
blown off the top of my head.
On a chance she'd be riding

in a car down the hill that day,
I stepped up, over my debris,
to the light of a diffident sky:

my crossover time, latent blue,
a dressing of cirrus. I took off
my tee shirt, an unlikely act

of courtship if she happened by,
looking over by choice not
chance at me mowing the same

patch of lawn over and over
in front of the clumped cedars,
an offering of my unrehearsed

goods in early summer, time
holding on to its first whisper
of assent, on a burnished day.

A POEM FOR JANE
1963

The mountain top is many years away
as we begin our mountain climb of love
from green and fertile land below.
We have a high and lifetime way to go.

Above the timberline we come upon
a silent land where nothing grows.
The bones of others who have come this way
are paired in mounds of total gray.

Before we level at the utmost height,
we make a perfect counterpoint of white.
The green beneath is many years ago;
now we must make our peace with snow.

INTERLOPER

FOR JANE AFTER FOUR YEARS

Somewhere between the birth and death of love
when every act or thought is morning gray,
an interloper in disguise will come
to shape disaster of our greenery.

At first we will not recognize his aim
and welcome him as cause enough for each
to wreck the other for the sake of love
while he will celebrate his broken child.

Before we learn to wear his Janus-face
as mask against compounded wrong on wrong,
we must see him for what he is
and must slay him for what we are.

Double Passage in Mid-Life
1987

In the hollows of the bed we lie still
but for the tremble that will not rock
the frame, too hunted by the day
to shape the night as we once told
our bodies how to act their roles.

Our breathing overcomes our breath
and so we drift into the dream
of faceless enemies, unremembered,
if they meant us harm at all
or if they played us far too well.

You turn to face the windowed light.
I turn to fit the contour of your life.

A Night on the Road

In a large room in the only motel open
past midnight this side of Chesapeake,
I turned side to side, nudged Jane to see
if she was awake. She wasn't but said,
What's wrong? and I said, *I can't sleep.*
She turned her head toward the wall.

The door to our room opened. Guests
without baggage came in, sprawled
out on the floor as if in a shelter, high
winds battering their homes, water rising
like a tide of death to claim what's left
behind, abandoned, all lost this night
to dark cacophonies of body and soul.

In the middle of the floor, sitting cross-
legged, a woman burned two candles.
Scents rose like desire, like first love.
When I woke to the first rush of light,
Jane was awake and always had been.
I told her about my dream and she said,
It's the oysters. In the air, wisteria.

Through an Upstairs Window

Winter, and the last of the sun drips
down the front of the brick two story
I see through a hole in the hardwoods,
up the hill in back and across a road.
Wind like a brush sweeps the branches.

Winter sits like a whimsical judge
on swift flights to Florida, Arizona:
forgiving streets and soft laws, par
three golf with six clubs in carts
on flat courses, but I hear Jane call

to me up the noiseless stairs. Good.
Time for my daily ration of bourbon,
time to talk the day down from its
loose abstractions, to take strict tally
of our cases won, lost, or pending.

Weddings

At a large wedding
on a rooftop thousands
of feet up, a girl asked

me a question I cannot
remember. That was
before I got up for the

first time, waking Jane
but not purposely. The
beams of our flashlights

crossed. Back in bed
I told her of my dream.
She said she dreamed

we were going to remarry
and we chose the gown
and tuxedo together. I

said, *How old were you?*
She said, *A lot younger.*
No surprise that we're

getting into each other's
dreams on nights like
this: much commerce in

the dark, close quarters
for sleepers on the move.

Room by Room

Room by room we are taming
this house built sideways
and close to a narrow street
with mailboxes in a row
like decoys on a midway,
just as we have been tamed
by a figure in the shadows
as darkness corners dusk.

And as we walked sideways
on a beach, wind offshore
and stiff like our joints,
I asked you if you wanted
to live there and you could
not hear me, so I asked again,
louder, so loud I screamed,
Why are you hiding from me?

Sound Waves

Some days I listen for Jane slowly opening
a drawer downstairs, a gentle sign,
proof she did not collapse, strike her head
on the counter top, fall to the floor, dead,

leaving me alone in a tub of tepid water,
soaking in an empty house. That thud—
it must have been an earthquake
or my neighbor blowing up another stump.

Other days I must close my ears, slide
underwater, where sounds float clearly,
and listen for the truth. Lifting the phone
off the hook, she speaks as if nothing happened.

Dress Codes

You're wearing the same dress
to church again, the blue cotton
with a lace collar. You say it fits
your mood and lets your body breathe,

and wonder why I even mention it,
as if I've been put in charge of dress
codes this morning, one day since
you've come back from Sally's bedside

to your mother's mind slipping further
out of sight. Your father says he'll
tend to her himself, for better or worse.
There's more of worse to come for both

of you. Circles darken under your eyes.
Your head throbs, drooping your lids.
It's that time when you've become
mother and child all over again.

When you were asleep last night,
you asked me, as if it were day,
"What's bothering you?" I lay there
astonished and said, "Nothing at all."

Part Two

Flight Patterns

I asked you if living at the end of a runway
bothers you. No answer, but you were asleep,
of course, and slept through the jumbo cargo

jet from Germany—abundant car parts,
maybe cars, too—at three a.m., when most
planes are ferrying drugs from south Florida,

their props breathing hard over the mountain
range north of us, like a lost platoon of tourists
hacking away at the underbrush once the rain

returned with a welcome vengeance.
That's what I thought before I woke up again,
to listen, always listen, to your quick breaths.

The Prize

Assigning points and adding them up
provide the proof required to award
the pumpkin of the year, in costume.
If we win, if we are blessed this way,

and if you insist we should escort it
to the ball, we'd better stand in line
at dawn, camping out in our pajamas,
an adventure. That's very important,

but only if the pumpkin cooperates.
As expected, the prize evaporated,
like the flight I dream I can never
board because I cannot find the gate.

I hope you're able to sleep in peace
without aching or a neighbor scaling
the bushy side of our house, an attack
on our unprotected flank, which is what

flanks are for, aren't they? Be careful.
Last night they egged your old car again,
the shame of our street, your legacy, my
luck, our past with plush blue upholstery.

Mirrors

In a doctor's office while
I wait for Jane's test results,
I look into the mirror, notice
for the first time in my life

I am smiling like my father,
broadly and slightly forced,
as if we've been caught trying
to enter a secure zone without

IDs, trespassers, unknown
to a guard whose hand is doing
a slow dance around his holster.
Out in the hall, as if on orders,

a nurse keeps closing the door
I keep opening, so I try to flash
her my new smile, as if it might
make a difference, as if I could

do something to face up to this
crack in my mirror image, this
news now slowly coming to light
in pictures at the end of the hall.

At the Kitchen Table

I'm holding onto the edge of the table
while you line up your pills
and six almonds, and I'm thinking
of how it was for you before
your body gave in to its legacy.

If I were you, I would ask me,
Why are you holding onto the table?
as if the seas are fifteen feet, the others
at our sitting back in their cabins,
having forgotten to take their pills.

Which is what I'm focusing on now—
the pills of our history, as we sit here,
one window blind breaking the sun
into chunks of light, as even as time,
like bands of gold on the table.

Tic Tacs

Three times this week
you've dropped the Tic Tacs,
wedging them between
your seat and its track,
and each time I tell you
to be more careful,
to put them in a side pocket,
when you remind me
there isn't one in my midget car,
asking me each time,
why do I get so upset
over Tic Tacs
while you adjust your scarf
to the wind, and snap on
the dark glasses we bought
at the ophthalmologist's,
and I'm thinking, as I shift
into reverse, why do I get
so upset over Tic Tacs,
and what am I supposed
to do if I want a Tic Tac,
and what will I do
if your heart closes up
like a sundrop after dark?

Sounds of a Late Afternoon

Jane's been sleeping for an hour,
and I think I hear running water
over the whoosh of air in my den:
her cells replenished, refreshed,

whatever happens after the very
sick, having weakened in the late
afternoon, fall asleep and awaken.
I think I hear her steps in the hall,

coming to where I am pretending
to read but thinking, Is that you?
I was reading a smart and funny
poem by David Kirby. Earlier,

I read of two Americans having
won the Nobel Prize in medicine
for learning how the sense of smell
works, as in knowing perfumes

or fine wines, not the cheap stuff
I drink after Jane's nap, as we sit
in the parlor and wait for a timer
to tick our supper down: she's

feeling the best of all day and I'm
drinking a tart, fruity chardonnay.
I ask, *How's the coffee?* She says,
Fine, her face bright, eyes perky:

sleep, the health machine, having
its set of overriding commands.
But she's still asleep, so I'll wake
her once I finish reading the poem

I drifted away from, in one of his
thirty, maybe forty line sentences,
brought that far by a movement
like familiarity, lifeline to a past.

Saying These Things

Today the sun sets for the last time in two months
on Barrow, Alaska, all that darkness, all that
turning on of lights to shine on the familiar, on
boots that hang from hooks in stark mudrooms.

In the mad corridors of perpetual night, I imagine
the drugstore turning off its lights for the duration:
Gone South for the season. Be back with the sun.
All my prescriptions, called in at the last minute,
snoozing in the in-basket, like last year's receipts.
The tingling in my hands and feet spreads like hives,
and I can hear my T-cells cracking like dead limbs.

Here, in the hospital room without a bed, waiting
one more time for Jane to return, I take my pulse
to the bold clock on the far wall, its strong black
numbers perfectly normal, its second hand sweeping
the terrain like radar. No weather in sight, and I am
saying these things because I am holding on to her life.

Jane

It is your time of diminishments:
loss of hair, the spine and pelvis
gone soft and cracking. White
blood cells savage and deplete

you like schoolyard bullies, like
cannibals of blood. Last night
while I was stroking your head,
you woke up just long enough

to say you heard your mother
calling out your name, twice.

Foreplay

We are lying in bed reading.
Before we turn off the lights,
I tell her I think my right
eye's going bad, and she says,
I'm sorry, without dropping
a line. Then I say, *I think
I may be getting an abscess*,
and she responds predictably.

If I look closely enough,
I will see her fragile veins
exploding beneath the skin's
surface, and the fine texture
of white hair that barely
covers her scalp. If I listen,
I will hear her kidneys pump
hard in a shallow bath of blood.

When she falls asleep, I will
slip in behind her eyes, listen
for her dreams to call to her,
to transport her to a room full
of strangers, where she will
draw quick, short breaths.
When she wakes up, her heart
will race, her cheeks will burn.

What I Can Do from Here

Like depth charges, your bottles of pills
line the deck of our breakfast room table,
and like a radio beacon gone haywire
on foggy nights, I repeat, over and over,

When will it ever end? You always say,
Try to find something to be happy about.
I am happy to practice my cottage magic:
to conjure up the morning you will rise

to silence in your limbs, your companion,
pain, having died in the phenomenal night,
and dance across the hot coals of our room,
saying to me, *Get up! We have things to do.*

Surgical Waiting Room

The surgical waiting room at St. Francis
is like a sports bar: TV alcoves for groups
of singular mind, leather and cloth chairs.
If some patrons seem to regard the screens
without passion, they deceive, and when
their eyes rim with red, they squint to pierce
the film that blurs whatever is happening:
severe droughts in the southwest and west,
athletes like gods threatening to strike
in mid-season. A surgeon in uniform sits
next to a woman, holds her hand, speaks
slowly, clearly, as if she does not understand
and she does not. A cleaning woman dusts
TVs with a long feather duster like a wand.
It's magic we need, and I need to disappear
through the double doors down the long hall,
wait for you to wake up, tell you absurd
stories until you move a hand, open an eye.

The Breakdown

I broke down in front of Jane on the day
           before
my birthday, after ten years of her no-cure
           illnesses,

with three plus years of rougher times,
           then hospice.
After a few wines, I wept, not an often act,
           which is OK,

because I reached some sort of threshold;
           and as we held
each other, I said, *What am I going to do
           when you die?*

and she responded, as if she would never die,
           and that, hey,
we still had each other, and let's make the best
           of it now

in our almost fifty years of being together, so
           finally,
I calmed down, not unhappy that I got it out.
           But, well,

enough—and the next day, on my birthday,
           as I was filling
my gas tank at a convenience store, the pump
           overflowed

onto my soiled car, and the clerk came outside,
           thinking
that surely I had done something wrong, which
           I had not.

He was as much help as a mole in a rock garden;
           and when he kept
howling, *What happened? What'd you do to it?*
           I said,

What the hell's wrong with you? Then at CVS
    I got a back spasm
from trying to juggle too much in too few arms
    and spent

the next two hours at home resting in bed,
    while Jane
and our daughter, Sally, went to the market
    to buy dinner,

and later, as Jane was sleeping off that effort,
    I set the table
for us, all the while knowing the truth about
    myself.

Golden Anniversary

Last night I saw Jane, if not for the first time,
                close to it,
with two other girls her age, walking in a park
                or a square
in a town none of us knew. I was eighteen,
                and instead

of being shy around girls, afraid of rejection,
                I tried
to get her attention, talk with her, ask her out,
                and, wow,
she started to walk toward me. Before we spoke
                she smiled

just as I woke up, with her sleeping next to me,
                breathing;
and I remembered her telling me yesterday,
                I may not
be able to make it to our 50th, and I did not
                answer

but I changed the subject on the spot by saying
                quickly,
I'm glad we can't still smell that dead squirrel;
                then
I said to her (I think I did), *If you feel OK later,*
                let's get out.

A Clearing Over Caesars Head

When I have more than two glasses of Chardonnay,
                I am different:
funnier, more friendly, more open, saying more
                than I should
about what I would have kept to myself
                a few years back,
and forgetting most of what I've said, until Jane
                reminds me,

when she thinks she should, or if I ask her to,
                and then I say,
Well, your memory isn't what it used to be, either,
                what with
all the pain medication and other pills of all shapes
                and colors
for her heart, which is closing up and her kidneys,
                which are

shutting down, and she replies, *You forget, too*;
                and we argue
for the first time in our union over who's right,
                the basis
for arguments anywhere, and I remember the poet
                William Stafford's
Right has a long and intricate name and the saying of it
                is a lonely thing,

while our own words divide us into distant halves—
                two memories
lost as in a gray smog over the Blue Ridge Mountains,
                until the winds
shift for both of us, and, in the distance, a clearing over
                Caesars Head,
where there is no right or wrong, just the trace for us
                of a blue mist.

The Frame

Your two by three inch picture taken for the church
                keeps falling
off a filing cabinet in my den, not because it is
                unsteady,

but my cabinet is littered with books, bills, notes—
                well, not littered
exactly—but enough so that anyone could let
                your frame fall

or slip behind my cabinet and its metallic twin.
                Your picture
is supposed to be next to the one Ray Barfield
                took of me in 1988,

ten years before yours, but, together, we seem
                alike in years,
if one considers us a pair, yet you are radiant
                in a blue halo,

smiling then, as if you had nothing to worry about,
                even after you took ill,
knowing you never had any odds to go up against:
                head cocked,

a strand of pearls highlighting your long neck,
                in a dress
of flowered print. I will remember you like that,
                even though

your light plastic frame is cracked and almost as
                unstable
as both of us in the morning, still finding our way
                to each other.

THE HAND

I was trying to find my way in the dark, not
                sure
of where I was but thinking I needed to find
                the hallway
to the front of my house; and when I could not,
                I fingered
and shuffled to somewhere, when, uh oh,
                I felt a hand,

and when I held it, it grabbed mine, as if
                they were
taking a walk or in the movies, and then life,
                like a slow reflex,
took over, and only then I realized it was Jane's
                small hand,
twitching over the side of our bed as she slept,
                while I was

looking for a hallway that had never been
                in our
small house; and as our hands locked, I knew
                I was
on her side of the bed, in the dark, in a house
                not mine,
but the house of a dreamer or a sleepwalker,
                if there is

any difference. I woke (I think) and told Jane
                she saved
my life, as she had done so often before. Finally,
                awake,
I found my flashlight, turned it on, all the while
                wondering,
Did I ever find what I was looking for, or was I
                never lost?

South on the Interstate

I am driving down the Interstate at 85 mph,
                trying to get
a specimen to the lab before it evaporates,
                or does
something to invalidate its reading, and then,
                well,
How do I explain to the doctor, or worse,
                to Jane

what I failed to do when all the steps
                are so
patently clear a child could follow them?
                Meanwhile,
the interstate on this stretch is full of cops:
                highway patrol,
sheriff's office, transportation police, and
                what else

in unmarked cars, and what if I'm stopped?
                Am I supposed
to say I'm trying to get a specimen to the lab
                before it's too late,
that the medical world needs to know? O Christ,
                keep my
arthritic hands on the wheel and my right foot
                where

it's supposed to be. What's that behind me,
                a Crown Vic,
from Vermont going south with a ski rack
                or a cop?
So I'm nervous, but so what? What else can
                I do
but *drive*, as Creeley wrote, *look out where*
                yr going.

A Blessing

for Jane on her 70th birthday

If my right hip aches when I first lie down,
I turn to face Jane, who always faces me
since her left side is a corridor of pain,
and as she drifts into a sedated sleep,

both of her hands twitch, as if a spirit
of unknown origin entered her frail body.
She holds my left wrist in her thin fingers,
as if to convince me of some belief, that

this is how it should be, or else she plays
in earnest with the fingers of my right hand,
so I cup her hand leisurely in mine, closing
it slowly, feeling her tremors until my hand

calms hers, and I whisper, *Time to sleep;*
and as she does, I count interludes between
breaths, longer than ever before but steady,
then release her, knowing how blessed I am.

Allergic Reaction

Almost dark in December and Jane
is napping off her pain, my time
to read a poem on *Lucia* at the Met
and sniffle, sneeze, nearly tear up,

not at the poem, which is funny, or
the opera, which is not, but at what-
ever coexists with the warm air
that tunnels through my ductwork.

Every spring the *Ducts R Me* man
places in my mailbox his grisly ad
of the life that inhabits our ducts,
and I think of the bodily debris

a Kirby Vacuum Cleaner man once
deposited on our living room rug,
in his free demonstration just after
Jane took ill, and now I am too far

removed from the arts to reconnect.
What I need is a new box of Kleenex,
clear passage through my mine field
of minutia, and Jane to awake happy.

Waking Up Tired

Rising later now, I wake more tired than before,
                when I used to walk
to the sky brightening and the frantic chirping
                of birds, squirrels.

The lines on my face deepen, linger longer,
                its T-cells
worn down by too many passages, too many
                revolutions,

while dreams once lost to time's generosity
                follow me,
as when, in the wide living room of an airplane
                that flew

in circles through narrow ways, I looked out
                at our wing—
or was it our tail or nose—that barely missed
                the green edge

of a building, and maybe that is why I wake tired:
                too much
of the active life asleep, or too little, as I think
                of you sleeping

on one side all night and part of the day, fingers
                involuntarily
touching my back, as if to send me a message,
                That it's OK,

your faint heart is beating and that, if you awake,
                so will pain,
as it always does, one throb following another.
                Should I count

your pain a blessing, as I do waking up tired late
                in the morning,
with you still lying next to me, now stirring, still
                holding on?

Night Calls

I woke to the ring of the telephone, which was
                not ringing,
then to Jane's soft, low voice calling, *Ron, Ron!*
                as she slept,

so I sat right up, asking, *What's the matter?*
                She never replied
but buried her head further into the pillow;
                then I knew

at this early hour in the treacherous morning
                what form
my dreams would take, if ever I fell asleep:
                not the usual

frustration of not being able to find my room,
                or my car,
or my way through absolute dark. Oh no,
                and I knew

if I slept I would awake to a day barely light,
                to her pain
in hushed moans, to her life slipping away
                from me,

no matter what I do or say or pray for silently
                behind doors,
my head bowed, my fingers interlocked so tight
                they bruise.

Dark House
February 17, 2009

In this dark house, after everyone has left,
                I walk
the halls with a flashlight, not to inspect
                        the doors
to see if they are locked but to secure
                        a passage,

since things move in the dark, only to return
                      by day
to their places, without a sign of undoing,
                        and I need
to think clearly, which is becoming harder.
                        Who came?

A nurse, an aide, a social worker, a pastor,
                      my children,
a grandson? If I have left one or more out,
                        what matters?
Look, a table is dancing in the middle of my
                      living room,

caught in the act of disobedience, or, well,
                      perhaps,
too strong a word, for in the dark one needs
                      a license
to tell here from there, so now I will look
                      in on Jane,

asleep in a hospital bed, more restless now.
                    Is it a sign
she would like to join me in my searching,
                      when I want only
to climb into her bed and take what will come
                      to us, together?

Pain

When Creeley wrote, *Pain is like a flower,*
               like this one,
like that one, he got it right, the pain
               starting
small, a seedling, then breaking into bud,
               followed
by a flower, the pain; and if I have wronged
               Creeley

I am sorry, but, yes, it is like that with pain,
               and only
one living with pain knows what he means,
               the pain
that is Janus-faced, bringing us together,
               sometimes
for the last time, or keeping us apart, what
               with

the storehouse of narcotics at our service.
               Sure,
Why not? Whatever the reason, why live
               like this,
like that, as when Hospice put a hospital bed
               in our room
because Jane wanted to die at home, and her
               pain

was so deep she could not even think or talk,
               full of morphine,
and I held her head, with her eyes closed,
               and I said
slowly, *What do you want me to do for you?*
               She rose
abruptly, saying, *Love me*, then lay back
               unconscious.

Fear and Love

Three-thirty on a Saturday afternoon when
                Jane woke up,
came down the hall to where I was sitting
                in my den,
reading poems by Matthew Dickman,
                then by
David Kirby, asking me, *When did you leave*
                the bed?

She is sleeping more these days and rising
                later in the day—
after noon today and then back to bed
                for a short nap.
If we had a dog or a cat, I am wondering
                when it would
come between us and growl or hiss when
                I took a step

toward her, or lie on my spot on the bed,
                refusing to move
so long as Jane was asleep or resting,
                its eyes
glazed with fear and love, its heart ready
                to spring
out of its body, knowing what we do not
                know

or believe, or what we refuse to accept
                in our anxiety,
or ignorance, or calculated innocence,
                while the cat
at Hospice House stood like a border guard
                at the front door
all day on the day that a patient was going
                to die.

Roots

This is not a hospital.
I tried not to emphasize the word,
so I said,
It is a place for you to rest,
a Hospice House.

But there it was—
the word
pandering to its root.

In the distance, behind the shades,
I heard someone sweeping a patio.
Why, when it was winter and who
looked at empty flower beds? Maybe,
here and there, a weed poked its head
through cracks in the stones, took
a deep breath and froze in the night.

Jane and Ronald Moran at their wedding reception
in the Vanderbilt Hotel, New York City, Jan. 31, 1959

The couple in their backyard: late 1980s

Part Three

LINES OF DEMARCATION
FEBRUARY 23, 2009

This is how it happened, so I am writing
                      lines
of demarcation for a day without tropes,
                      in Room 122
of the Hospice House in Simpsonville, SC.
                      I had

to leave Jane alone in her room for two hours.
                      When
I returned, she was on her back, her mouth
                      wide open
as before, but her thin and bruised body
                      did not twitch.

She was still, like a figure in a photograph,
                      not gasping
for breath as when I last left her room.
                      I tried to close
her right eye, barely open, but it would not
                      stay shut.

The nurse said, *Do you want a few minutes*
                      alone with her?
I said, I'm OK, which I was not, but I only knew
                      later
how much I was not OK and never would be
                      again.

In Place of a Prayer

Last night, when my self-indulgence was running
                    spectacularly high
as I lay in bed, holding out my arms, as if posing
                    for a Bronzino,
while I was begging Jane to absolve me of guilt,
                    to accept

my apologies, to let me know that I would be
                    all right,
that I need only one more sign of her presence
                    to quell
my insecurities, I heard three chirps three times
                    in a row

that came from a bird, I suppose, in the waste area
                    out back—
decaying maples, sludge, ivy, dens of snakes—
                    by law
a flood zone; and so I sat up in bed, knowing I was
                    forgiven

for what I did or did not do while she was dying
                    next to me,
and I thanked her for saving my life, one more time,
                    as she always had,
and I vowed never again to ask her to overcome
                    her death.

The Reprimand

I saw an old man tottering on his front stoop,
                so I asked him,
What do you want? and he swung the cane
                he did not have
at me, and I knew exactly what to get for him.
                I pulled out

a pint of bourbon from my oversized pocket,
                and we sat
on his stoop with a small swarm of termites,
                and drank.
When I emptied the pint, I went inside, fell
                into a dream

of Jane looking at me sternly and saying,
                What?
if it was a dream, or maybe that was enough
                to rouse her
from her long sleep, to warn me, *No, No.*
                Not that way.

Mother and Daughter

The bond between mother and daughter can be
                so profound
that when Jane died, Sally died, too, differently
                and elsewhere—

more secret yet more telling than the casket or urn,
                or grave—
a not wanting to touch, much less see,
                the final

resting place of Jane, or the sweater she wore
                whenever
the temperature dropped enough for the heat
                to kick on,

or talk about Jane to anyone, just ordinary talk.
                What they liked
to do together, Sally did for Jane as she could
                before Jane

wore down: feet shuffling, unable to breathe
                without
pain, without a nitro placed under the tongue.
                All this, then,

was filed so deeply in Sally's consciousness
                that nothing
would surface on its own; and if it did, well,
                what good

would it ever do for her, whose life had been
                a testament
to fending off a precise cooling, like a sweater
                in early fall.

Killing Time

With my ten self-imposed minutes to go,
                I had
to stop whatever I was doing to kill time,
                get up,
begin to do something else that would take
                more time

to complete—with clearly not enough left
                to finish,
so I started on something else, only to quit
                and worse,
to forget I ever began it—when my watch
                said,

Let's go, and I was always ready then,
                back when
Jane was alive, so I would seek her out,
                as she combed
her white hair or slipped on a bracelet,
                and ask her,

When are you ever going to be ready to go?
                She would say,
Pretty soon or *In a minute,* or when agitated,
                Don't push!
and where were we going that was so crucial:
                the drugstore,

supermarket, ATM? Now when the countdown
                begins,
I walk through a quiet house, looking at clocks,
                checking
my watch, and leave the house early, always
                too early.

The Wait

I am waiting now, more than before, when I sat
        in my den
in the afternoons, listening for Jane to awaken—
        to hear water
being turned on—or for twilight to arrive,
        like a pawn
to the sun's trajectory, or even for a cloud base
        to drift down
the Blue Ridge range, or for the time I needed
        to lay out her pills.

Now that she is dead, I am almost alert to what
        happens,
such as a light bulb burning out, so I can limp
        upstairs
to find a replacement, and if there is none,
        well, then,
here's the event I have waited for all day:
        the drive
to and from CVS or Publix or Ace Hardware,
        wherever

I need to go to fulfill my mission of the day,
        my purpose.
Meanwhile another jet bound for GSP is making
        its final approach
in my airspace, probably a commuter, such as
        a Comair CRJ-900.
But why does it sound as if it's coming from,
        not going to GSP?
When WHOMP, it falls into my front yard,
        miraculously

with no one injured; and as the occupants slide
        down a chute,
Look! There's Jane, as she was in the good days,
        and I try
to move toward her, to call to her but I cannot;
        and as she walks
to the bus to take her where the jet could not,
        she looks my way,
smiles, waves, and says to me, as I read her lips,
        I'll wait for you.

Living Space
May 2, 2009

Even friends, my middle-aged kids, and
        their spouses
still avoid my living room, where we all
        once gathered
while Jane was alive and able. So now
        we crowd

my den or sit packed on a sagging couch
        in the parlor.
O dear Jesus, when will it end, and will I
        ever stop
thinking of not being a better caregiver
        when her drugs

took over some functions? This small,
        lovely woman
in her wingback chair—pale, eyes mostly
        clear—
while I sat in the upholstered orange chair
        of my parents,

interrupting, at times, to correct a small error,
        until I realized,
What difference could it possibly make if
        her world
tipped out of round from theirs, when right
        is hard

enough to figure out without complications;
        the long
sleeve of injustice covering up wrist bone,
        thumb bone,
knuckle bones while I am still trying to make
        it right—

to tell her, *I was wrong to criticize you*—
        my weakness—
all my chits called in as if long overdrawn,
        guilt a streamer
like the tail of a comet never to be found,
        but out there.

Letters to Jane
April 23, 2009

Thank you for helping to guide me through
           the two months
since you died by answering my supplications
           in forms
I understand, as in the dream where I tried
           to find you
 without disturbing others in a store by calling
           your name

too often or loud, and you woke me, saying
           Ron!
as if you found me, the lost one wandering
           the aisles;
or the morning when I woke up late, light
           everywhere,
and I heard you exhale a long, healthy sigh
           next to me,

my best day since you left: no ropy webs
           to untangle,
no urge for self-pity, and everywhere I went
           I met the good;
then the one night, late, when I begged you
           to assure me,
Yes, I am still with you, however you chose;
           and knowing

my love of airplanes, you sent a twin-engine
           turboprop
very low over our house, on a landing pattern
           rarely used.
Tomorrow Sally and Harry are coming for a drink
           at five,
and I think they will bring Nikki along with them.
           Love.

June 15, 2009

Two days ago would have been your 71st
    birthday,
so I bought a red rose, and the florist, a man
    with bags
under his eyes the size of golf balls, knowing
    I had

a long drive to the grave, wrapped the rose
    on his own
in white, delicate paper, tying it neatly with
    a thin bow.
Nancy, the co-owner of the cemetery, washed
    our marker,

placing the rose where I thought it should be,
    and I took
a picture. Driving home I remembered I forgot
    to say a prayer.
It has been like that since you died, even before,
    but more now,

as when I think all day it is Saturday, when it is
    Friday
or Monday, or when I walk straight to a room
    with a purpose
that on the journey drifts out of cognition.
    Do you

remember the black, spiny caterpillars hanging
    in sacs
off the live oak and pecan trees in our backyard
    in Baton Rouge?
No one walked barefoot outside in their season,
    and why

would a caterpillar need spines? To ward off
    those birds
with huge beaks in the subtropics? Remember
    when one
caterpillar, loosed from its sac, fell off a leaf
    onto your

bouffant hair? Should I write every day as I did
              when
we courted, our airmail letters crisscrossing
              over Memphis
or maybe the blunt band of the Blue Ridge?
              I miss you.

Trying to Stay Alive

It came to that, after reading all the good,
        the bad numbers.
Who wouldn't concur with your insistence
        on staying alive?
The slow walk through years, like blood
        thickening,

coagulating, the taking of step by step
        blindly into
all manner of bodily distress, for which,
        even now,
they have not yet found the right words,
        much less

a clue as to how to relieve the suffering,
        whatever
form it takes, like the death bed rattle
        for breath
when the body deep inside cries out
        for life,

to hang on just this much longer, like
        an inmate
on death row trying to bargain for life
        with
the priest, but no such luck, not with
        the curtain

drawn, and the gallery as solemn as
        the priest;
and, my one love, I am so sorry to have
        failed you
in a way that mattered to you, not in
        the absence

of care but in the absence of my grasp
        that this
is how it had to be, no matter what either
        of us
wanted, no matter how much we tried
        together.

On Going to See a Bereavement Counselor for the First Time on an Afternoon in Mid-July, 2009

I have driven this road before, perhaps a dozen times,
                and each time

I nearly missed the awkward turnoff to the Hospice House
                where Jane died

months ago, and whose face of death was like a piece
                of sculpture

that over time will never change, even minutely,
                as in a lip

bitten by the wind or hair styled by acid rains. I know
                why I must go,

even though I will leave unchanged, even less aware
                of what

I can never forgive, and knowing that one more person
                will know

what I have not done and try to justify my inadequacies,
                my only

way of responding at the time to the vagaries of blood,
                the knotting

of memory. Not before its time can one be promised
                closure.

The Language of Holding Up

This is the time they ask, *How are you holding up?*
Druggist, nurse, pastor, the kid who shovels snow,
and others you may hardly know or recognize,
but they know and they ask, and all you can say,

or are expected to say, is *OK. Doing the best I can.*
Meanwhile the checkout clerk at the supermarket
asks, *How are you today?* and you say *Fine. And You?*
These questions and their abbreviated replies beg

to be interpreted—as in, *What does Fine mean?*
Or *What is OK?* Besides a semi-literacy for *all right*,
however you spell it. All along, whatever the meaning,
faucets drip at slow intervals on a very cold night.

Trying to Make Peace

Now that I am alone I am trying to make peace
                    with my world,
not as in the greening of my life but, rather,
                    as in the harmony
with which I hope will exist between the objects
                    of my life
and me, since we inhabit the same dwelling
                    and depend

on each other for mutual respect and, well, love,
                    if that is not
too strong a word, not for me but maybe for them,
                    even though
with only minor interventions have we ever had
                    reason
to doubt the intentions of the other, as in the steps
                    in the garage

and a bottle of wine conspiring to floor me.
                    Above me
the ceiling fan whirrs in my small den, its blades
                    much too large
for the cubic footage, and it wobbles, as if it is
                    uncertain
about continuing to play its role; and elsewhere
                    other fans,

are gathering like a cabal, giving me some doubt
                    and little leeway
about how to quell their insecurities, much less mine,
                    unless I bought
new fans, custom made for each of the five rooms
                    in which
they hang, my life and anyone else's maybe at stake,
                    or not,

depending on my misreading of or paranoia about
                    the inanimate.
If Jane were still here the fans would hum to her wish
                    to cool down,
no questions asked, no wobbling, no grim concerns,
                    and as for
the rest of the house and property, small as it is,
                    the same.

Pillows

This is where I have failed, in not valuing
                pillows
in the living room or parlor, the room
                where
we once served tea, cakes, and cookies
                to strangers,

like new neighbors, or our daughter's
                first date—
a twitchy boy in hard pressed chinos,
                Sally
in a white, airy sundress, on a clear night
                in June.

That was then, and pillows were only
                to relieve
one's back, so that when I went shopping
                to defeminize
my house—a word my daughter tossed
                and I caught—

the sofas and chairs all wore pillows like
                overcoats,
and when I sat down to try one on, I put
                pillows
on the floor, or on top of each other, until
                I realized,

I am supposed to admire the pillows, not
                sit down,
so I turned to the salesperson, *Say what?*
                Not sit?
which concluded my effort at that store
                to defeminize

a house I never thought of as feminine,
                only as
Jane's house, since decorating was never
                in my
skill-set, and I felt comfortable wherever
                she was.

November 23, 2009

So I am wandering around my house now
        without
my cane, a feat requiring over two months,
        trying
for the third time today to find where I left
        my pen,
and in the process counting the dents
        in my soft

hardwood floors. If my eyes were better
        I would
see too much of what is or what is not
        there,
nine months from the day Jane died,
        alone
in a room at Hospice House, while I was
        on a break.

Maybe I will try to go outside without
        my cane,
look for the squirrel traps on and around
        my house;
and if I see one caught, if I think of setting
        it free,
I will remember, last year, when maggots
        and flies

let loose a toxicity that began to drown
        Jane's lungs,
so I turned away, called in the small captive
        to Critter Control.
O Christ, What a life I have made for myself
        since then.

Learning How

When my eyes and hands were pitcher and catcher,
                I would toss
a ball up with my right hand while holding the bat
                in my left—

clearly unorthodox—but I could hit it, or a crabapple
                or small stone,
whatever offered itself to a twelve year old with no
                league in sight,

the only games being one-a-cat or pickups on fields
                we cut
to size, rocks for bases, the woods for long and lost balls.
                In my dreams

I cannot hit anything, no matter what my hands hold;
                and when
I wake up, I keep thinking of E. M. Forster's *Only connect,*
                and all I want

is to rerun my life with Jane, beginning in June, where
                under
an oak in Walnut Hill Park, we both asked, *Can it work?*
                Yes, it did.

A Note on the Author

Ronald Moran was born in Philadelphia and moved to New Britain, Connecticut, when he was 10. He received his BA from Colby College and his MA and PhD from Louisiana State University. After having taught at the University of North Carolina for nine years, he joined the Clemson University faculty in 1975, and retired twice, first in 1998 and then in 2000. He served in a number of positions at Clemson, including Professor and Head of the Department of English, Associate Dean, and Interim Dean. In 1969-70, he was Fulbright Lecturer at the University of Würzburg in Germany. He has published eleven books/chapbooks of poetry, including *Saying These Things*, the inaugural volume of poetry issued by the Clemson University Digital Press in 2004. Moran is the author of one book of literary criticism and co-author of another. His poems and essays are widely published in magazines such as *Commonweal, Emrys Journal, Evening Street Review, The Louisiana Review, Main Street Rag, Mankato Poetry Review, North American Review, Northeast, Northwest Review, Pudding Magazine, South Carolina Review, Southern Review, Tar River Poetry*, and *Yankee*. Moran lives in Simpsonville, South Carolina. His work is archived in the James B. Duke Library at Furman University.

www.ingramcontent.com/pod-product-compliance
Lightning Source LLC
Chambersburg PA
CBHW031127160426
43192CB00008B/1138